Keeping Your Relationship Spicy

A 12-Month Guided Workbook for Couples Who Want to Intensify the Spice in Their Relationship!

Annette Crittenden

Keeping Your Relationship Spicy

Publisher note: This guided workbook is based on personal experiences and research. The author is not a certified relationship specialist or a sex therapist.

Copyright © 2020 by Books by Annette C

All rights reserved: This book is protected by the copyright laws of the United States of America. No part of this book may be reproduced in any form or by any means, electronic or mechanical, including photocopying, recording, informational storage or retrieval systems, without written permission by the author, except where permitted by law, for the purpose of review, or where otherwise noted.

Published by:

Books by Annette C

www.BooksByAnnetteC.com

Editing By:

Gloria Green and Victoria Smith

ISBN for print version:

9798639575136

First Edition

Printed in the United States of America

Dedication

This book is dedicated to my deceased parents T.F and Gerlean Brown. Your memories are reflected in my creativity.

Andrew Moses (deceased) who told me I could be anything I wanted to be and he believed in me (bright-eyes).

Special Thanks to:

Kevin Crittenden, my loving husband, for always pushing me to be the best.

Laticia Austin for spending many work hours on FaceTime pushing me to finish my guided workbook and giving me business advice.

Traffic Sales & Profit w/Lamar Tyler for motiving me during TSP Live to go out and do anything I wanted to do. Lamar and his wife are constantly creating motivating events to encourage people to follow their dreams and ideals to profit.

Crystal Swain-Bates for the Journal Challenge. The tips and tricks she gave were invaluable.

Gloria Green for keeping my book in focus after she proofed the book.

Family and friends who always have been in my corner no matter what I am doing.

Introduction

Is your relationship as spicy and exciting as it was when you were dating? Can some spice be added to your relationship?

Do you feel like your relationship is loveless? Have life activities such as careers or children gotten in the way of some of things you use to do in your relationship.

Keeping Your Relationship Spicy is an interactive journal designed to help readers add or intensify their relationship. There are questions that both participants must answer.

You will take a trip down memory lane to the beginning to focus on why you chose your mate. Activities are directed to open communications.

The journal can be completed in 12 months or more, it is totally up to you and your mate. This journal can be utilized over and over again.

Open the book and enter a world of questions, games, and activities. Date nights that occur inside and outside the house. Tap into your sensuality and sexual fantasies.

Are you ready? If you are, open the book!

Contents

Month One 10
    Completion Agreement 11
    Up to 52 Dates 12
    Week 1 - Attractions 14
    Week 2 - Role Play Scenarios...16
    Week 3 - Sexual Positions..18
    Week 4 - Love Making Spots...20

Month 2...22
    Are you Ready to Date?..24
    Week 1 - Favorite Music...26
    Week 2 - Favorite Outfit...28
    Week 3 - Unique Places..30
    Week 4 - Role Play - Replay 32

Month 3...34
    Are you Ready to Date?..36
    Week 1 - Compliment of the Day...38
    Week 2 - Gratitude of the Day..40
    Week 3 - Sensual Touch Spots..42
    Week 4 - Love Making Spots - Replay 44

Month 4...46
    Are you Ready to Date?..48
    Week 1 - Bedtime Stories...50
    Week 2 - 20 Questions (Sexual and Intimate Thoughts).................52
    Week 3 - Pick Me Up 54
    Week 4 - Candlelight Night..56

Month 5 58
Are you Ready to Date? 60
Week 1 - Sexy Scavenger Hunt.. 62
Week 2 - Sexy Texts.. 64
Week 3 - Watch Me Undress 66
Week 4 - Role Play - Replay... 68

Month 6 70
Are you Ready to Date? 72
Week 1 - Food in the Bedroom 74
Week 2 - Trip to Sex Store (Physical or Online)................................ 76
Week 3 - Sexy Pictures (With Clothes) 78
Week 4 - Massage Me 80

Month 7 82
Are you Ready to Date? 84
Week 1 - Bath Time 86
Week 2 - Kiss Me 88
Week 3 - Sexy Looks 90
Week 4 - Touch Me Just Because 92

Month 8 94
Are you Ready to Date? 96
Week 1 - Movie Night... 98
Week 2 - Strip Game Night 100
Week 3 - Let's Cook Together 102
Week 4 - Love Making Spots - Replay... 104

Month 9 106
Are you Ready to Date? 108
Week 1 - Sexy Hand-Written Note 110
Week 2 - Picnic in the House... 112

- Week 3 - Let the Eyes Talk ... 114
- Week 4 - Role Play - Replay ... 116

Month 10 ... 118
- Are you Ready to Date? ... 120
- Week 1 - Talk Dirty to Me ... 122
- Week 2 - Feed Me ... 124
- Week 3 - Sexual Toys ... 126
- Week 4 - Love Making Spots - Replay ... 128

Month 11 ... 130
- Are you Ready to Date? ... 132
- Week 1 - Call Me from Another Room ... 134
- Week 2 - Attraction through Media ... 136
- Week 3 - Cuddle Time ... 138
- Week 4 - Undress Me ... 140

Month 12 ... 142
- Are you Ready to Date? ... 144
- Week 1 - Love Making Spots - Replay ... 146
- Week 2 - Love Making Positions – Replay ... 148
- Week 3 - Role Play - Replay ... 150
- Week 4 - Keeping your Relationship Spicy Recap ... 152
- About the Author ... 154

Let the spice begin!

Are you Ready?

Month One

Completion Agreement

I agree to complete this workbook to best of my ability. I agree to be:

- Honest
- Open-minded
- Committed
- Negotiable to my mate's ideas!

After completing manual, I agree to continue the activities to keep my relationship spicy.

The workbook contains four weeks of activities per month.

Commit to setting a date on your calendar each week to do the activities together.

Signatures

_____   Date: _____

_____   Date: _____

Up to 52 Dates

Life sometimes gets in the way of couples going on dates. Our careers take away hours from us and make us tired at the end of the day. We become comfortable with our normal routine.

The goal of this exercise is to plan 52 dates. You may not be able to take all 52 dates, but plan them. This guide can be used for years to come.

At the beginning of each month, each person plans 2 dates each for the month. Use your creative imagination when planning the ideal date. Go to Google Search and type in "ideal date night" to retrieve tons of ideas.

Suggestions:

- Dinner date
- Comedy Show
- Jazz Club
- Aquarium

Each month concentrate on these dates and share them with your mate. Read each one together and discuss which ones to take.

Get ready to experience 52 exciting dates.

Mate 1 – Dates for the Month

First Date

Date: _____ Time: _____

Destination: _____

Second Date

Date: _____ Time: _____

Destination: _____

Mate 2 – Dates for the Month

First Date

Date: _____ Time: _____

Destination: _____

Second Date

Date: _____ Time: _____

Destination: _____

Week 1 - Attractions

Write down what is your attraction to your mate. Dig deep inside yourself and really think about your mate including both physical and non-physical qualities.

Suggestions:

- The time you met
- The conversations you had
- The dates
- Do he/she make you laugh
- What thought of them makes you smile
- What is it about that person that draws your attention to them when they enter the room?
- What is about that person that brings out the animalistic nature (lust) in you?

Concentrate on these traits and share them with your mate. Read each one together and discuss them.

Some of these traits may have started and have stopped for whatever reason; not knowing they meant something to either of you.

The week is dedicated to bringing back that loving feeling and that initial spark.

Getting you ready for 52 weeks of spice and fire in your relationship.

Mate 1 – List of Attractions

Date: _____

- ❖ _____
- ❖ _____
- ❖ _____
- ❖ _____
- ❖ _____

Mate 2 – List of Attractions

Date: _____

- ❖ _____
- ❖ _____
- ❖ _____
- ❖ _____
- ❖ _____

Week 2 - Role Play Scenarios

Have you ever wanted to role play?

Example. You are the doctor and your mate play the patient. The 'doctor' has to examine every part of their 'patient's' body to make sure they are okay. Use tools to explore and explain as you 'examine'. Use your own made up technical terms to bring the most excitement to your 'patient'.

Write down what you would like to role play.

Research is available on the internet. Dig deep into your thoughts for that fantasy land that all of us have.

Suggestions:

- Doctor – Patient
- Teacher – Student
- Athlete – Cheerleader
- Drill Sergeant – Private
- Dirty Cop – Nasty Street Walker
- Master – Sex Slave

Concentrate on these roles and share them with your mate. Read each one together and discuss them. Delete any if both cannot agree to participate.

Practice one role from each person this week.

The week is dedicated to tapping into your creativity and wild side.

Elements in the exercise are also used later in the workbook.

Mate 1 – Role Play Scenarios and Descriptions

Date: _____

- ❖ _____
- ❖ _____
- ❖ _____
- ❖ _____
- ❖ _____
- ❖ _____
- ❖ _____
- ❖ _____
- ❖ _____
- ❖ _____
- ❖ _____
- ❖ _____

Mate 2 – Role Play Scenarios and Descriptions

Date: _____

- ❖ _____
- ❖ _____
- ❖ _____
- ❖ _____
- ❖ _____
- ❖ _____
- ❖ _____
- ❖ _____
- ❖ _____
- ❖ _____
- ❖ _____
- ❖ _____

Week 3 - Sexual Positions

Have you ever wanted to explore different sexual positions?

Write down what positions you want to explore.

Research is available on the internet. Go to Google Search and type in "sex position" to retrieve tons of ideas. Dig deep into your thoughts for that fantasy land we all have.

Suggestions:

- **Corkscrew** – Your mate is near the edge of a bed resting on the hip and forearm of one side and pressing their thighs together to allow a tighter grip. Your partner stands and straddles you, entering from behind.
- **Doggy Style** - Get on all fours, then have your partner enter you from behind, with his upper body straight up or slightly draped over you. Meet each other's stokes. Use your hand to stimulate the clitoris.
- **Reverse Cowgirl** – Your mate sits in a chair. You straddle him backwards; lean forward and rest your hands/or elbow on a table/chair; or rest your hands on the floor. Depending on how low can you go for the ride!

Concentrate on these positions and share them with your mate. Read each one together and discuss them. Mark out any if both cannot agree to participate.

Practice one position from each person this week.

The week is dedicated to tapping into your open mind.

Elements of the exercise are used later in the workbook.

Mate 1 – Sex Positions and Descriptions

Date: _____

- ❖ _____
- ❖ _____
- ❖ _____
- ❖ _____
- ❖ _____
- ❖ _____
- ❖ _____
- ❖ _____
- ❖ _____
- ❖ _____

Mate 2 – Sexual Positions - Descriptions

Date: _____

- ❖ _____
- ❖ _____
- ❖ _____
- ❖ _____
- ❖ _____
- ❖ _____
- ❖ _____
- ❖ _____
- ❖ _____
- ❖ _____

Week 4 - Love Making Spots

What is your favorite love making spot?

Write down loving making spots you know or want to get to know.

Research is available on the internet. Go to Google Search and type in "Places to have sex" to retrieve tons of ideas. Dig deep into your thoughts for that fantasy land that all of us have.

Suggestions:

- On a Beach
- In a tent – either in the middle of your yard or while camping.
- Kitchen
- Park
- Car at a Drive-in Movie Theater
- Public Bathroom
- Underneath an overpass
- In a closet (pretend you are locked in)
- Sit on him, in the garage, with the sunroof open

Concentrate on these love making spots and share them with your mate. Read each one together and discuss them. Mark out any if both cannot agree to participate.

Have sex in one spot from each person list this week.

The week is dedicated to tapping into your daring side.

The elements in the exercise are used later in the workbook.

Mate 1 – Love Making Spots and Descriptions

Date: _____

- ❖ _____
- ❖ _____
- ❖ _____
- ❖ _____
- ❖ _____
- ❖ _____
- ❖ _____
- ❖ _____

Mate 2 – Love Making Spots and Descriptions

Date: _____

- ❖ _____
- ❖ _____
- ❖ _____
- ❖ _____
- ❖ _____
- ❖ _____
- ❖ _____
- ❖ _____

Month 2

Did you enjoy last month?

Are you ready for another fantastic month of activities?

If you are ready, turn the page and let the spice begin!

Are you Ready to Date?

Did you enjoy your dates last month?

It is time to plan your next month of dates. Use your creative imagination when planning the ideal date. Go to Google Search and type in "ideal date night" to retrieve tons of ideas.

Suggestions:

- Short train ride going nowhere and back
- Attend a festival in a neighboring city
- Choose a new restaurant that neither of you have tried
- Have a game night
- Mystery trip – plan a day or afternoon to drive nowhere, just stop if you see something of interest or to eat
- Volunteer together – at a food kitchen or Habitat for a day

Concentrate on these dates and share them with your mate. Read each one together and discuss which ones to take.

Get ready to experience more exciting dates.

Mate 1 – Dates for the Month

First Date

Date: _____ Time: _____

Destination: _____

Second Date

Date: _____ Time: _____

Destination: _____

Mate 2 – Dates for the Month

First Date

Date: _____ Time: _____

Destination: _____

Second Date

Date: _____ Time: _____

Destination: _____

Week 1 - Favorite Music

In this exercise each person will write down what is your favorite music. Dig deep inside yourself and really think about your favorite music growing up till now.

When completing this section, think about:

- Music that gets you dancing
- Music you and your mate enjoy
- Slow music
- Fast music
- Thinking music
- Calming music

Concentrate on music and share it with your mate. Read each one together and discuss them.

Listen to some of the music and get up and dance to it.

The week is dedicated to bringing the love for music back into your relationship

Dance the night and day away.

Mate 1 – Favorite Music with Artist

Date: _____

- ❖ _____
- ❖ _____
- ❖ _____
- ❖ _____
- ❖ _____
- ❖ _____
- ❖ _____
- ❖ _____

Mate 2 – Favorite Music with Artist

Date: _____

- ❖ _____
- ❖ _____
- ❖ _____
- ❖ _____
- ❖ _____
- ❖ _____
- ❖ _____
- ❖ _____

Week 2 - Favorite Outfit

In this exercise each person will list what is your favorite outfit you like to see your mate wear.

Dig deep inside yourself and really think about all the outfits your mate has worn and what you want them to wear. Use the internet or catalogs to find outfits. Take a trip to the closet.

When completing this section, think about:

- Sexy Teddy
- Tight Jeans
- Suit
- Just underwear

Concentrate on outfits and share it with your mate. Read each one together and discuss them.

Wear an outfit or two that was listed for each other this week.

The week is dedicated to bringing back the feeling you get when you see your eye-candy walk in the room in your favorite outfit.

Let the googling eyes begin.

Mate 1 – Favorite Outfits and Descriptions

Date: _____

- ❖ _____
- ❖ _____
- ❖ _____
- ❖ _____
- ❖ _____

Mate 2 – Favorite Outfits and Descriptions

Date: _____

- ❖ _____
- ❖ _____
- ❖ _____
- ❖ _____
- ❖ _____

Week 3 - Unique Places

Are you adventurous or curious? Is there something you wanted to do and have not done it?

Research is available on the internet. Go to Google Search and type in "fun activities" to retrieve tons of ideas. Dig deep into your thoughts for that fantasy land that all of us have.

Suggestions:

- Paintballing
- Painting with a Twist
- Ripley's Believe It or Not
- Watch the sunset

Concentrate on these unique places and share them with your mate. Read each one together and discuss them. Delete any if both cannot agree to participate.

Agree to go to one or two unique places this week.

The week is dedicated to tapping into your uniqueness.

Mate 1 – Unique Places with Descriptions

Date: _____

- ❖ _____
- ❖ _____
- ❖ _____
- ❖ _____
- ❖ _____

Mate 2 – Unique Places with Descriptions

Date: _____

- ❖ _____
- ❖ _____
- ❖ _____
- ❖ _____
- ❖ _____

Week 4 - Role Play - Replay

It is time to role-play again – Take a look at your list from the first month and pick a role or look for additional roles.

Remember the Example. You be the doctor and your mate be the patient and you have to examine every part of their body to make sure they are okay. You use tools to explore and explain as you go. You use your own made up technical terms to bring the most excitement to your partner.

There is still time to do some research on the internet. Go to Google and enter 'Sexual role play' for tons of ideals. Dig deep into your thoughts for that fantasy land that all of us have.

Suggestions:

- Pretend your mate is a cop and you are trying to talk/suggest your way out of a ticket
- Pretend he is your professor and you want to 'persuade' him/her to give you a better grade
- You are a nurse and want to give the patient a sponge bath
- Pretend your mate is your Uber drive and give him an 'other' type of payment
- Pretend your mate is your prisoner; tie him/her up and have your way with them

Practice one role from each person this week.

The week is dedicated to re-tapping into your creativity and wild side.

Mate 1 – Role Play – Replay

What are your choices? New? First Month?

Date: _____

- ❖ _____
- ❖ _____

Mate 2 – Role Play – Replay

What are your choices? New? First Month?

Date: _____

- ❖ _____
- ❖ _____

Month 3

Did you enjoy last month?

Are you ready for another fantastic month of activities?

If you are ready, turn the page and let the spice begin!

Are you Ready to Date?

Did you enjoy your dates last month?

It is time to plan your next dates. Use your creative imagination when planning the ideal date. Go to Google Search and type in "ideal date night" to retrieve tons of ideas.

Suggestions:

- Take an Adult Shop field trip
- Plan a progressive date – drinks one place, appetizer another, dessert at yet another
- Attend an Erotic Storytelling Event
- Check into a fancy hotel room
- Go to a sex club – you don't have to participate if you don't want to – you can be a voyager
- Prepare an Aphrodisiac Buffet and feed each other

Concentrate on these dates and share them with your mate. Read each one together and discuss which ones to take.

Get ready to experience more exciting dates.

Mate 1 – Dates for the Month

First Date

Date: _____   Time: _____

Destination: _____

Second Date

Date: _____   Time: _____

Destination: _____

Mate 2 – Dates for the Month

First Date

Date: _____   Time: _____

Destination: _____

Second Date

Date: _____   Time: _____

Destination: _____

Week 1 - Compliment of the Day

Often, we think kindly about our mates and we never let the words come out of our mouth because we think they already know how we feel.

Everyone loves a compliment when it is sincere.

Write down and express your feelings. Dig deep inside yourself and really think about your mate. In your list include both physical and non-physical compliments.

Suggestions:

- I love your smile because...
- Cologne or Perfume
- His/her style because...
- Being with you is fun because...

Concentrate on complimenting your mate.

The week is dedicated to bringing back that loving smile back to her/his face.

Get ready to see those smiles across her/his face.

Mate 1 – Compliments for the Week (7 Days)

Date: _____

- ❖ _____
- ❖ _____
- ❖ _____
- ❖ _____
- ❖ _____
- ❖ _____
- ❖ _____

Mate 2 – Compliments for the Week (7 Days)

Date: _____

- ❖ _____
- ❖ _____
- ❖ _____
- ❖ _____
- ❖ _____
- ❖ _____
- ❖ _____

Week 2 - Gratitude of the Day

We are thankful for what our mates do for us, or to us, and we never let the words come out of our mouth because we think they already know how we feel.

Most people do things without ever expecting to get a thank you. A thank you or a statement of gratitude is always welcome.

Write down and express your feelings to your partner. Dig deep inside yourself and really think about your mate. In your list include both physical and non-physical gratitude.

When completing this section, think about:
- You are the best
- Thank you for breakfast this morning
- I appreciate you taking out the trash

Concentrate on showing gratitude to your partner and seal it with a kiss.

The week is dedicated to continuing to bring back that loving smile to her/his face.

Get ready to see those smiles continue across her/his face.

Mate 1 – Gratitude of the Day (7 Days)

Date: _____

- ❖ _____
- ❖ _____
- ❖ _____
- ❖ _____
- ❖ _____
- ❖ _____
- ❖ _____

Mate 2 – Gratitude of the Day (7 Days)

Date: _____

- ❖ _____
- ❖ _____
- ❖ _____
- ❖ _____
- ❖ _____
- ❖ _____
- ❖ _____

Week 3 - Sensual Touch Spots

When was the last time you experienced a sensual touch?

Write down in what spots you like to be touched.

Dig deep into your thoughts for that fantasy land that all of us have.

Suggestions:

- Soft gentle touches
- The nape of the neck
- Shoulders
- Soft kisses on the lower back
- For men, little licks or soft sucking on the ridge below the head of the penis (the frenulum)
- Foot massage
- Gentle kisses behind your mate's knees

Concentrate on sharing these sensual touches with your mate. Mark down each touch that your mate really enjoys and the others that are not so effective, but add to the event.

Practice as many sensual touches as possible this week.

The week is dedicated to getting to know your partner's body.

Mate 1 – Sensual Touches - Descriptions
Date: _____

- ❖ _____
- ❖ _____
- ❖ _____
- ❖ _____
- ❖ _____
- ❖ _____

Mate 2 – Sensual Touches - Descriptions
Date: _____

- ❖ _____
- ❖ _____
- ❖ _____
- ❖ _____
- ❖ _____
- ❖ _____

Week 4 - Love Making Spots - Replay

It is time to explore love making spots again – Take a look at your list from the first month and pick a spot or look for additional spots to explore.

There is still time to do some research on the internet. Go to Google Search and type in "Places to have sex" to retrieve tons of ideas. Dig deep into your thoughts for that fantasy land that all of us have.

Suggestions:

- On the balcony of a hotel room with a gorgeous view
- In the bed of a truck filled with blankets
- In an open field beneath the stars on a warm night
- On the top of a pool table
- Against a tree in a park; you can be a loud as you want to be

Have sex in one spot from each person's list this week.

The week is dedicated to tapping into your daring side.

Mate 1 – Love Making Spots and Descriptions - Replay

Date: _____

- ❖ _____
- ❖ _____

Mate 2 – Love Making Spots and Descriptions - Replay

Date: _____

- ❖ _____
- ❖ _____

Month 4

Did you enjoy last month?

Are you ready for another fantastic month of activities?

If you are ready, turn the page and let the spice begin!

Are you Ready to Date?

Did you enjoy your dates last month?

It is time to plan your next month of dates. Use your creative imagination when planning the ideal date. Go to Google Search and type in "ideal date night" to retrieve tons of ideas.

Suggestions:

- Go back to where it all began
- Go to a petting zoo
- Find a weird museum to go to
- Write out the story of how we met and fell in love
- Plan to catch a sunrise or a sunset

Concentrate on these dates and share them with your mate. Read each one together and discuss which ones to take.

Get ready to experience more exciting dates.

Mate 1 – Dates for the Month

First Date

Date: _____ Time: _____

Destination: _____

Second Date

Date: _____ Time: _____

Destination: _____

Mate 2 – Dates for the Month

First Date

Date: _____ Time: _____

Destination: _____

Second Date

Date: _____ Time: _____

Destination: _____

Week 1 - Bedtime Stories

Time to use the bedtime story imagination. Dig deep inside yourself and really think about your mate.

You can choose to complete this exercise in one or two ways:

Read erotic stories to each other that both of you agree on.
OR
Create your own story and let your partner create it with you.

Example of creating a bedtime story:

Partner one starts:

- Amanda lets the water roll down her body in the shower. Her thoughts went to last week's activities they had to do on love making spots. She lets her hand run down her body.

Partner two continues:

- Mark watches Amanda from the cracked bathroom door. Ever since the couple purchased the Keeping Your Relationship Spicy guide book their relationship had changed and he could not wait to get home every day.

Concentrate on sensual bedtime stories. Read the story, act out the parts of the stories that interests you.

The week is dedicated to your sexual imagination.

Mate 1 – Bedtime Stories - Ideas

Date: _____

- ❖ _____
- ❖ _____
- ❖ _____
- ❖ _____
- ❖ _____
- ❖ _____

Mate 2 – Bedtime Stories - Ideas

Date: _____

- ❖ _____
- ❖ _____
- ❖ _____
- ❖ _____
- ❖ _____
- ❖ _____

Week 2 - 20 Questions (Sexual and Intimate Thoughts)

Have you ever played 20 questions? There are several variations of the game.

Rules of the game:

- Questioner – Ask question about something sexual or sensual places, objects (i.e., body part) or persons.
- Partner – Response to each question with a 'Yes' or 'No' or a one-word answer.
- Game twist – Questioner can touch parts of body as he/she ask the question if it helps his/her question.

Dig deep into your thoughts for that fantasy land that all of us have.

Suggestions:

- Questioner – Do you enjoy phone sex?
- Answer - Yes

Concentrate on getting to truly know your mate's intimate thoughts to generate passion.

20 Questions

List some of the places, objects, or person that were used.

Date: _____

- ❖ _____
- ❖ _____
- ❖ _____
- ❖ _____
- ❖ _____
- ❖ _____
- ❖ _____
- ❖ _____
- ❖ _____
- ❖ _____

Week 3 - Pick Me Up

Do you remember when you met?

Do you remember where you first met?

Do you remember what they were wearing?

Create a situation where you pretend you are meeting your mate for the first time. Think of ways to introduce yourself to your mate over and over again.

This activity can be part of one of your dates this month.

Suggestions:

- Meeting at a backyard barbecue
- Meeting at a house party (your house – music playing)

Concentrate on picking up your partner and bring back that dating feeling.

The week is dedicated to bringing back the dating feeling.

Mate 1 – Pick Me Up Scenarios

Date: _____

- ❖ _____
- ❖ _____
- ❖ _____
- ❖ _____
- ❖ _____
- ❖ _____

Mate 2 – Pick me Up Scenarios

Date: _____

- ❖ _____
- ❖ _____
- ❖ _____
- ❖ _____
- ❖ _____
- ❖ _____

Week 4 - Candlelight Night

When was the last time you enjoyed a candlelight night?

Write down what you think would be an enjoyable candlelight night.

This activity can be part of one of your dates this month.

Research is available on the internet. Dig deep into your thoughts for that fantasy land that all of us have.

Suggestions:

- Turn off all the lights in the room and light LED or real candles for a Candlelight Night – add your favorite music
- Candlelight Night Bathtub – light candles (LED or real) all over the bathroom. Fill the tub with sensual bubble bath soap and rose petals. Have a bottle of champagne or wine with glasses on a tray
- Arrange a sexy candlelight picnic in your backyard

Concentrate on creating a candlelight night for you and your partner. The night can be as simple or complex as the imagination takes you.

The week is dedicated to tapping into your romantic side.

Mate 1 – Candlelight Night Scenarios

Date: _____

- ❖ _____
- ❖ _____
- ❖ _____
- ❖ _____
- ❖ _____
- ❖ _____

Mate 2 – Candlelight Night Scenarios

Date: _____

- ❖ _____
- ❖ _____
- ❖ _____
- ❖ _____
- ❖ _____
- ❖ _____

Month 5

Did you enjoy last month?

Are you ready for another fantastic month of activities?

If you are ready, turn the page and let the spice begin!

Are you Ready to Date?

Did you enjoy your dates last month?

It is time to plan your next dates. Use your creative imagination when planning the ideal date. Go to Google Search and type in "ideal date night" to retrieve tons of ideas.

Suggestions:

- Let him/her indulge you – run a bubble bath and let your mate bathe you slowly all over
- Dress sexy; go to a bar/club first and let your mate 'pick' you up
- Go somewhere or do something unconventional – try a new cuisine; go test drive that expensive car you will never buy
- Go to a baseball. football, basketball game, any kind of sports game together and eat the junk food

Concentrate on these dates and share them with your mate. Read each one together and discuss which ones to take.

Get ready to experience more exciting dates.

Mate 1 – Dates for the Month

First Date

Date: _____ Time: _____

Destination: _____

Second Date

Date: _____ Time: _____

Destination: _____

Mate 2 – Dates for the Month

First Date

Date: _____ Time: _____

Destination: _____

Second Date

Date: _____ Time: _____

Destination: _____

Week 1 - Sexy Scavenger Hunt

Wikipedia definition: A scavenger hunt is a game in which the organizers prepare a list defining specific items, which the participants seek to gather or complete all items on the list, usually without purchasing them. The goal is to be the first to complete the list or to complete the most items on that list.

Create a scavenger hunt for your partner. Think of your mate and sensual and sexy turn on that lead to endless excitement.

Dig deep inside yourself and really think about your mate. In your ideas include both physical and non-physical activities.

Suggestions:

- Clue # 1 – You are excellent at selecting this delicious beverage. (Answer is bottle of wine hidden in the fridge)
- Clue # 2 – You really know how to whip things up in the bedroom (Answer: Whip Can) that can be used in the bedroom – place in a shopping bag to carry with you till the end of the challenge
- Clue # 3 – An item in the kitchen cabinet that is also as sweet and chocolate like you. (Answer – Hershey Syrup)

This week concentrate on the romantic creative side that everyone has inside them.

The week is dedicated to imagination and creativity.

Mate 1 – Sexy Scavenger Hunt

Date: _____

- ❖ _____
- ❖ _____
- ❖ _____
- ❖ _____
- ❖ _____
- ❖ _____

Mate 2 – Sexy Scavenger Hunt

Date: _____

- ❖ _____
- ❖ _____
- ❖ _____
- ❖ _____
- ❖ _____
- ❖ _____
- ❖ _____

Week 2 - Sexy Texts

When was the last time you sent or received a sexy text?

In this exercise each day send your mate sexy and intimate texts.

Dig deep into your thoughts for that fantasy land that all of us have.

Suggestions:

- I almost did not let you out the door with that outfit you had on this morning
- I can't believe how out of control I feel sometimes when I think about you.
- What is the hottest thing I can do for you when I see you?
- I can't stop thinking about you and me…and what you did to me last night…damn!

Concentrate on coming up with a sexy text for each day of the week.

The week is dedicated to bringing smiles and giggles to your mate face.

Mate 1 – Sexy Texts (7-Day Week)

Date: _____

- ❖ _____
- ❖ _____
- ❖ _____
- ❖ _____
- ❖ _____
- ❖ _____

Mate 2 – Sexy Texts (7-Day Week)

Date: _____

- ❖ _____
- ❖ _____
- ❖ _____
- ❖ _____
- ❖ _____
- ❖ _____

Week 3 - Watch Me Undress

Has your mate ever undressed for you?

Think of ways to undress for your mate.

Dig deep into your thoughts for that fantasy land that all of us have.

Suggestions:

- Sensual music playing while undressing
- Dress up – to undress
- Sexy night wear

Concentrate on undressing for your mate ideas. Release all hidden inhibitions about the body when naked during this exercise.

Undress for your mate this week using the ideas written.

The week is dedicated to falling in love with your mate's body all over again.

Mate 1 – Watch Me Undress

Date: _____

- ❖ _____
- ❖ _____
- ❖ _____
- ❖ _____
- ❖ _____
- ❖ _____

Mate 2 – Watch Me Undress

Date: _____

- ❖ _____
- ❖ _____
- ❖ _____
- ❖ _____
- ❖ _____
- ❖ _____

Week 4 - Role Play - Replay

It is time to role-play again – Take a look at your list from the first month and pick a role or look for additional roles.

Remember the Example. You be the doctor and your mate be the patient and you have to examine every part of their body to make sure they are okay. Use tools to explore and explain as you go. You use your own made up technical terms to bring the most excitement to your partner.

There is still time to do some research on the internet. Go to Google and enter 'Sexual role play' for tons of ideals. Dig deep into your thoughts for that fantasy land that all of us have.

Suggestions:

- The repairman and the homeowner – he came to fix your 'pipes'
- The stripper and the customer
- Role reversal – Let your man go to a bar/club early and you flirt/pick him up
- Client and the Call girl – Let your 'client' list exactly what he wants you to do
- Innocent vs Not so Innocent – One of you pretends to be a bit naïve and the other 'teaches' the first everything to do

Practice one role from each person this week.

The week is dedicated to re-tapping into your creativity and wild side.

Mate 1 – Role Play – Replay

What are your choices? New? First Month?

Date: _____

❖ _____
   _____

❖ _____
   _____

Mate 2 – Role Play – Replay

What are your choices? New? First Month?

Date: _____

❖ _____
   _____

❖ _____

Month 6

Did you enjoy last month?

Are you ready for another fantastic month of activities?

If you are ready, turn the page and let the spice begin!

Are you Ready to Date?

Did you enjoy your dates last month?

It is time to plan your next month for dates. Try some stay at home dates.

Use your creative imagination when planning the ideal date. Go to Google Search and type in "ideal date night" to retrieve tons of ideas.

Suggestions:

- Make a Blanket Fort – pretend the lights are out and use flashlights to eat and play
- Plan a dance night at home; dress up and have drinks and mood music
- Cook a Gourmet Meal together - With store-bought ingredients, a nice tablecloth and some candles, you can create a romantic evening in your own dining room.

Concentrate on these dates and share them with your mate. Read each one together and discuss which ones to take.

Get ready to experience more exciting dates.

Mate 1 – Dates for the Month

First Date

Date: _____ Time: _____

Destination: _____

Second Date

Date: _____ Time: _____

Destination: _____

Mate 2 – Dates for the Month

First Date

Date: _____ Time: _____

Destination: _____

Second Date

Date: _____ Time: _____

Destination: _____

Week 1 - Food in the Bedroom

Is food used in the bedroom?

In this exercise each person writes down what foods can enhance the experience in the bedroom.

Research is available on the internet. Go to Google Search and type in "food used in the bedroom" to retrieve tons of ideas. Dig deep into your thoughts for that fantasy land that all of us have.

Suggestions:

- Chocolate syrup – Spread the syrup over his/her chest like he/she is the yummiest piece of bread you've ever seen. Let loose the power of the tongue!
- Honey - I suggest you use it in combination with a sweetened cooking oil - lather his body with it (it could be a nice way to give him a massage; think of how you grease up your food just before you're ready to devour it). Next, let the honey just fall and drip. For best effects, do this standing, or sitting. Better still, on a kitchen counter!
- Ice cream - On each other's bodies. Take turns. Let him lay you down. And drop a dollop of chilled ice cream onto your navel. Then, let him eat it off you.

Concentrate on foods that can be used in the bedroom. Read each one together and discuss them.

Use an item(s) from each of your lists this week.

The week is dedicated to enhancing the sexual appetite.

Mate 1 – Food in the Bedroom

Date: _____

- ❖ _____
- ❖ _____
- ❖ _____
- ❖ _____
- ❖ _____
- ❖ _____

Mate 2 – Food in the Bedroom

Date: _____

- ❖ _____
- ❖ _____
- ❖ _____
- ❖ _____
- ❖ _____
- ❖ _____

Week 2 - Trip to Sex Store (Physical or Online)

When was the last time you made a visit to a sex store online or in person? Think about shopping as foreplay.

In this exercise take a trip to a sex store online line or to a physical store. In the store, explore the items that they sell that are known and unknown.

Write down the top 5 items of interest in the store for each person. Purchase one item per person, if affordable.

Suggestions:

- Warming massage oils
- Videos
- Flavored condoms
- Blindfolds

Concentrate on the sex store and share ideas with your mate. Read each one together and discuss them. Mark out any if both cannot agree to participate.

Practice with one item from each person this week.

The week is dedicated to tapping into looking outside the box for added pleasure.

Mate 1 – Sex Store Items

Date: _____

- ❖ _____
- ❖ _____
- ❖ _____
- ❖ _____
- ❖ _____
- ❖ _____

Mate 2 – Sex Store Items

Date: _____

- ❖ _____
- ❖ _____
- ❖ _____
- ❖ _____
- ❖ _____
- ❖ _____

Week 3 - Sexy Pictures (With Clothes)

Have you ever wanted to be a photographer for your mate?

Dress for photos taken with a camera phone or personal camera. Your partner is the photographer for the photo shoot. The poses taken are at the discretion of the photographer.

Research is available on the internet. Go to Google Search and type in "boudoir poses" to retrieve tons of ideas. Dig deep into your thoughts for that fantasy land that all of us have.

Suggestions:

- Mate's shirt with shorts
- Sexy night wear
- Dress up (sexy dress or suit)

Concentrate on photos (outfits and poses) and share them with your mate. Read each one together and discuss them. Mark out any if both cannot agree to participate.

Take photos of each other this week.

The week is dedicated to tapping into your photographic side.

Mate 1 – Sexy Pictures (With Clothes)
Date: _____

- ❖ _____
- ❖ _____
- ❖ _____
- ❖ _____
- ❖ _____
- ❖ _____

Mate 2 – Sexy Pictures (With Clothes)
Date: _____

- ❖ _____
- ❖ _____
- ❖ _____
- ❖ _____
- ❖ _____
- ❖ _____
- ❖ _____

Week 4 - Massage Me

When was your last massage? What spots did you like massaged most?

Write down the spots you liked massaged most.

Research is available on the internet. Go to Google Search and type in "spots to massage" to retrieve tons of ideas.

Suggestions:

- Set the mood with mood lighting (e.g., scented candles, dimmers, etc.)
- Massage lotions, oils or waxes – Pour some oil on your hands and gently rub the warmed oil/lotion all over your lover's body in sensual, long strokes)
- Massage candle – Light the wick and when the wax melts, the candle will turn into a warm liquid that can be safely poured onto the skin for a sweet-smelling massage.
- Fingertips – Using your fingertips, trace the contours of your partner's body. Run your fingers through their hair, gently graze their neck with the pads of your fingers or follow the smooth curves of their lips with your thumbs.

Concentrate on spots to be massaged and share them with your mate. Read each one together and discuss them. Mark out any if both cannot agree to participate.

Massage a spot from each person's list this week.

The week is dedicated to tapping into your loving relaxation side.

Mate 1 – Massage Me - Spots

Date: _____

- ❖ _____
- ❖ _____
- ❖ _____
- ❖ _____
- ❖ _____
- ❖ _____

Mate 2 – Massage Me - Spots

Date: _____

- ❖ _____
- ❖ _____
- ❖ _____
- ❖ _____
- ❖ _____
- ❖ _____

Month 7

Did you enjoy last month?

Are you ready for another fantastic month of activities?

If you are ready, turn the page and let the spice begin!

Are you Ready to Date?

Did you enjoy your dates last month?

It is time to plan your next dates. Use your creative imagination when planning the ideal date. Go to Google Search and type in "ideal date night" to retrieve tons of ideas.

Suggestions:

- Make a movie – not that kind! Go to different locations around your neighborhood and make mini videos with your phone of you each letting loose with wacky dance moves or speaking in accents to strangers. Do silly interviews.
- Check out a nearby city you have never visited and just explore!
- Plan a Couple's Spa Day

Concentrate on these dates and share them with your mate. Read each one together and discuss which ones to take.

Get ready to experience more exciting dates.

Mate 1 – Dates for the Month

First Date

Date: _____   Time: _____

Destination: _____

Second Date

Date: _____   Time: _____

Destination: _____

Mate 2 – Dates for the Month

First Date

Date: _____   Time: _____

Destination: _____

Second Date

Date: _____   Time: _____

Destination: _____

Week 1 - Bath Time

Have you ever shared bath time with your mate?

Write down what items make bath time enjoyable for your mate. Dig deep inside yourself and really think about your mate.

Suggestions:

- Bubble bath vs shower
- Bath bombs
- Bath oils
- Soft music
- Candles

Concentrate on items to make your mate relax and enjoy the shower or bath. Read each one together and discuss them.

Bathe each other using one of each idea written.

The week is dedicated to bringing back that clean loving feeling.

Mate 1 – Bath Time Suggestions

Date: _____

- ❖ _____
- ❖ _____
- ❖ _____
- ❖ _____
- ❖ _____
- ❖ _____

Mate 2 – Bath Time Suggestions

Date: _____

- ❖ _____
- ❖ _____
- ❖ _____
- ❖ _____
- ❖ _____
- ❖ _____

Week 2 - Kiss Me

Did you know there are several types of kisses?

Write down how you like to be kissed.

Research is available on the internet. Go to Google Search and type in "types of kisses" to retrieve tons of ideas. Dig deep into your thoughts for that fantasy land that all of us have

Suggestions:

- French kiss
- Eskimo kiss
- Peck kiss

Concentrate on types of kisses. Read each one together and discuss them. Mark out any if both cannot agree to participate

Use the list and kiss your partner this week.

The week is dedicated to tapping into getting close and personal.

Mate 1 – Kiss Me

Date: _____

- ❖ _____
- ❖ _____
- ❖ _____
- ❖ _____
- ❖ _____
- ❖ _____

Mate 2 – Kiss Me

Date: _____

- ❖ _____
- ❖ _____
- ❖ _____
- ❖ _____
- ❖ _____
- ❖ _____
- ❖ _____

Week 3 - Sexy Looks

Did you know that you communicate by the way you look at someone?

Write down types of sexy looks that communicate the most to your partner.

Research is available on the internet. Go to Google Search and type in "sexy facial expression" to retrieve tons of ideas. Dig deep into your thoughts for that fantasy land that all of us have.

Suggestions:

- Wink
- Look deep into my eyes
- Kissy face

Concentrate on sexy looks and share them with your mate.

Practice your sexy looks on your mate and see how they respond.

The week is dedicated to non-verbal communication.

Mate 1 – Sexy Looks

Date: _____

- ❖ _____
- ❖ _____
- ❖ _____
- ❖ _____
- ❖ _____
- ❖ _____

Mate 2 – Sexy Looks

Date: _____

- ❖ _____
- ❖ _____
- ❖ _____
- ❖ _____
- ❖ _____
- ❖ _____

Week 4 - Touch Me Just Because

When was the last time you touched your mate just because?

Write down places you like to touch your mate.

Research is available on the internet. Go to Google Search and type in "sexual touches" to retrieve tons of ideas. Dig deep into your thoughts for that fantasy land that all of us have.

Suggestions:

- Holding hands
- Kiss on the neck
- Hug from behind

Concentrate on how to touch your mate.

Touch your mate in new ways this week.

The week is dedicated to tapping into getting close to your mate.

Mate 1 – List of Touches

Date: _____

- ❖ _____
- ❖ _____
- ❖ _____
- ❖ _____
- ❖ _____
- ❖ _____

Mate 2 – List of Touches

Date: _____

- ❖ _____
- ❖ _____
- ❖ _____
- ❖ _____
- ❖ _____
- ❖ _____

Month 8

Did you enjoy last month?

Are you ready for another fantastic month of activities?

If you are ready, turn the page and let the spice begin!

Are you Ready to Date?

Did you enjoy your dates last month?

It is time to plan your next dates. Use your creative imagination when planning the ideal date. Go to Google Search and type in "ideal date night" to retrieve tons of ideas.

Suggestions:

- Stay in and play board games together
- Redo a room together – paint, re-arrange furniture, etc.
- Take a dance class together
- Go bowling

Concentrate on these dates and share them with your mate. Read each one together and discuss which ones to take.

Get ready to experience more exciting dates.

Mate 1 – Dates for the Month

First Date

Date: _____   Time: _____

Destination: _____

Second Date

Date: _____   Time: _____

Destination: _____

Mate 2 – Dates for the Month

First Date

Date: _____   Time: _____

Destination: _____

Second Date

Date: _____   Time: _____

Destination: _____

Week 1 - Movie Night

When was the last time you enjoyed movie night with your mate?

Write down a list of movies you would like to see with your mate.

Suggestions:

- Dress Up! – go for something nice but cozy
- Set the scene – pillows, blankets, lighting
- Prepare gourmet popcorn / finger foods
- Great bottle of wine or other favorite drinks

Concentrate on movies that both parties can enjoy. Read each one together and discuss them.

Watch movies with your partner this week.

The week is dedicated to bringing back closeness, sharing, and togetherness.

Mate 1 – List of Movies

Date: _____

- ❖ _____
- ❖ _____
- ❖ _____
- ❖ _____
- ❖ _____
- ❖ _____

Mate 2 – List of Movies

Date: _____

- ❖ _____
- ❖ _____
- ❖ _____
- ❖ _____
- ❖ _____
- ❖ _____
- ❖ _____

Week 2 - Strip Game Night

When was the last time you played a game with your partner?

Write down a list of games to play with your mate.

Suggestions:

- Pictionary
- Bingo
- Monopoly

Concentrate on a list of games and share them with your mate. Read each one together and discuss them. Mark the ones you both agree to play.

Play games with your mate this week. When one-person loses a round he/she removes a piece of clothing till one person is totally naked.

The week is dedicated to tapping into your fun and game side.

Mate 1 – Strip Game Night

Date: _____

- ❖ _____
- ❖ _____
- ❖ _____
- ❖ _____
- ❖ _____
- ❖ _____

Mate 2 – Strip Game Night

Date: _____

- ❖ _____
- ❖ _____
- ❖ _____
- ❖ _____
- ❖ _____
- ❖ _____

Week 3 - Let's Cook Together

When was the last time you cooked with your mate?

Write down your favorite meal or meals you want to try.

Suggestions:
- Steak and Potato
- Lasagna
- Pot Pie
- Find a new recipe to try!

Concentrate on the meals that both parties will enjoy. Read each one together and decide which ones to cook.

Cook meals together this week.

The week is dedicated to your culinary side.

Mate 1 – List of Meals

Date: _____

- ❖ _____
- ❖ _____
- ❖ _____
- ❖ _____
- ❖ _____
- ❖ _____

Mate 2 – List of Meals

Date: _____

- ❖ _____
- ❖ _____
- ❖ _____
- ❖ _____
- ❖ _____
- ❖ _____

Week 4 - Love Making Spots - Replay

It is time to explore love making spots again – Take a look at your list from the first month and pick a spot or look for additional spots to explore.

There is still time to do some research on the internet. Go to Google Search and type in "Places to have sex" to retrieve tons of ideas. Dig deep into your thoughts for that fantasy land that all of us have.

Suggestions:
- Under a stairwell – while people are using it
- On an air mattress outside under the stars
- In an elevator that is not used much

Have sex in one spot from each person's list this week.

The week is dedicated to tapping into your daring side.

Mate 1 – Love Making Spots and Descriptions - Replay

Date: _____

❖ _____
   _____

❖ _____
   _____

Mate 2 – Love Making Spots and Descriptions - Replay

Date: _____

❖ _____
   _____

❖ _____
   _____

Month 9

Did you enjoy last month?

Are you ready for another fantastic month of activities?

If you are ready, turn the page and let the spice begin!

Are you Ready to Date?

Did you enjoy your dates last month?

It is time to plan your next dates. Use your creative imagination when planning the ideal date. Go to Google Search and type in "ideal date night" to retrieve tons of ideas.

Suggestions:

- Karaoke Night (even at home)
- A rotating restaurant that shows the entire city at night
- Take dance lessons – most clubs offer line dance lessons for free

Concentrate on these dates and share them with your mate. Read each one together and discuss which ones to take.

Get ready to experience more exciting dates.

Mate 1 – Dates for the Month

First Date

Date: _____ Time: _____

Destination: _____

Second Date

Date: _____ Time: _____

Destination: _____

Mate 2 – Dates for the Month

First Date

Date: _____ Time: _____

Destination: _____

Second Date

Date: _____ Time: _____

Destination: _____

Week 1 - Sexy Hand-Written Note

> Honey,
>
> I cannot imagine another second without you in my arms. Hurry home!
>
> Signed: Waiting 4 U

When was the last time you received a sexy hand written note from your mate?

In this exercise each person will write their mate sexy hand written notes and leave them in places for them to find.

Suggestions:

- The smell of your cologne or perfume makes me want to rip all your clothes off.
- Every time you touch me my heart races and my breath stop.

Concentrate on writing sexy notes for your mate.

Leave your mate sexy hand written notes where they can find them this week.

The week is dedicated to bringing back creativity and love.

Getting you ready to see the smiles on their face.

Mate 1 – Sexy Hand-Written Note Ideas

Date: _____

- ❖ _____
- ❖ _____
- ❖ _____
- ❖ _____
- ❖ _____
- ❖ _____

Mate 2 – Sexy Hand-Written Note Ideas

Date: _____

- ❖ _____
- ❖ _____
- ❖ _____
- ❖ _____
- ❖ _____
- ❖ _____

Week 2 - Picnic in the House

Have you ever had a picnic in the house?

Write down items that can be used to have a picnic in the house.

Suggestions:

- Blanket laid out in the biggest open space or backyard
- Swap water and soda for wine or sparkling wine
- Swap cookies for a fancy bar of dark chocolate
- Swap veggies and dip for a fresh herby salad
- Swap sandwiches for a charcuterie board featuring cured meats, different types of sliced bread and a variety of cheese, olives and honey

Concentrate on picnic ideas to allow and enjoy quality time with your mate. Read each one together and discuss them. Agree on the picnic for the week after the discussion.

Have a picnic in the house this week. The picnic could count toward one of your dates this month.

The week is dedicated to tapping into quality time creation.

Mate 1 – Picnic in the House Ideas

Date: _____

- ❖ _____
- ❖ _____
- ❖ _____
- ❖ _____
- ❖ _____
- ❖ _____

Mate 2 – Picnic in the House Ideas

Date: _____

- ❖ _____
- ❖ _____
- ❖ _____
- ❖ _____
- ❖ _____
- ❖ _____

Week 3 - Let the Eyes Talk

When was the last time you let your eyes convey what you were thinking to your partner?

Write down what you convey to your mate with your eyes.

Suggestions:

- I love you – a deep look with an award-winning smile
- Come here – a sexy look with a head nod

Concentrate on ways to sensually talk to your mate with your eyes. Talking with your eyes can help you when you are in a crowded room and want to get close to your mate without anyone else knowing what is going on.

Practice talking to your partner with only your eyes. You may use a few hand motions to really convey some messages.

The week is dedicated to connecting with your partner.

Mate 1 – Let the Eyes Talk Ideas

Date: _____

- ❖ _____
- ❖ _____
- ❖ _____
- ❖ _____
- ❖ _____
- ❖ _____

Mate 2 – Let the Eyes Talk Ideas

Date: _____

- ❖ _____
- ❖ _____
- ❖ _____
- ❖ _____
- ❖ _____
- ❖ _____
- ❖ _____

Week 4 - Role Play - Replay

It is time to role-play again – Take a look at your list from the first month and pick a role or look for additional roles.

Remember the Example. You be the doctor and your mate be the patient and you have to examine every part of their body to make sure they are okay. You use tools to explore and explain as you go. You use your own made up technical terms to bring the most excitement to your partner.

There is still time to do some research on the internet. Go to Google and enter 'Sexual role play' for tons of ideals. Dig deep into your thoughts for that fantasy land that all of us have.

Suggestions:
- Special Order – You make order for food and you are short on cash – how are you going to pay?
- Teacher – Student
- Star – I am your biggest groupie
- Stripper – Give me a lap dance, please

Practice one role from each person this week.

The week is dedicated to re-tapping into your creativity and wild side.

Mate 1 – Role Play – Replay

What are your choices? New? First Month?

Date: _____

❖ _____
  _____

❖ _____
  _____

Mate 2 – Role Play – Replay

What are your choices? New? First Month?

Date: _____

❖ _____
  _____

❖ _____
  _____

Month 10

Did you enjoy last month?

Are you ready for another fantastic month of activities?

If you are ready, turn the page and let the spice begin!

Are you Ready to Date?

Did you enjoy your dates last month?

It is time to plan your next dates. Use your creative imagination when planning the ideal date. Go to Google Search and type in "ideal date night" to retrieve tons of ideas.

Suggestions:

- Go get some dessert and feed each other
- Go bar hopping for the evening
- A night of playing pool or bowling

Concentrate on these dates and share them with your mate. Read each one together and discuss which ones to take.

Get ready to experience more exciting dates.

Mate 1 – Dates for the Month

First Date

Date: _____ Time: _____

Destination: _____

Second Date

Date: _____ Time: _____

Destination: _____

Mate 2 – Dates for the Month

First Date

Date: _____ Time: _____

Destination: _____

Second Date

Date: _____ Time: _____

Destination: _____

Week 1 - Talk Dirty to Me

When was the last time you talked dirty to your mate (made them blush)?

Write down ideas of what you want to talk dirty to your mate about. Dig deep inside yourself and really think about your mate.

Suggestions:

- The outfit you are wearing makes me want to rip your clothes off and take you on the table.
- Come over here and let me see if I can find that spot that makes you hot.

Concentrate on your dirty talk. What will make your make blush and be turned on at the same time?

The week is dedicated to bringing back heat that both of you share.

Mate 1 – Talk Dirty to me Ideals

Date: _____

- ❖ _____
- ❖ _____
- ❖ _____
- ❖ _____
- ❖ _____
- ❖ _____

Mate 2 – Talk Dirty to Me Ideals

Date: _____

- ❖ _____
- ❖ _____
- ❖ _____
- ❖ _____
- ❖ _____
- ❖ _____

Week 2 - Feed Me

Do you know how erotic it is to feed your mate?

Write down a list of finger foods that can be fed to your mate.

Suggestions:

- Wings
- Fruit
- Cheese
- Chips (Cheetos)

Concentrate on types of finger foods. Read each one together and discuss them to determine which ones to use.

Feed your mate this week. Choose foods that they can lick off your fingers if it is juicy or messy (i.e. wings).

Use those techniques from previous exercises to look into your mate.

The week is dedicated to tapping into making food sexy.

Mate 1 – Feed Me Ideas

Date: _____

- ❖ _____
- ❖ _____
- ❖ _____
- ❖ _____
- ❖ _____
- ❖ _____

Mate 2 – Feed Me Ideas

Date: _____

- ❖ _____
- ❖ _____
- ❖ _____
- ❖ _____
- ❖ _____
- ❖ _____
- ❖ _____

Week 3 - Sexual Toys

Do you use sexual toys in the bedroom?

Write down a list of sexual toys to use.

Research is available on the internet. Go to Google Search and type in "sex toys" to retrieve tons of ideas. Dig deep into your thoughts for that fantasy land that all of us have.

Suggestions:

- Clitoral Sucking Vibrator
- Silicone Dual Penis Ring.

Concentrate on toys that bring pleasure to both partners. Read each one together and discuss them. Mark out any if both cannot agree to participate.

Use one of the sex toys from each list this week.

This week is dedicated to playing with sex toys.

Mate 1 – Sex Toys List

Date: _____

- ❖ _____
- ❖ _____
- ❖ _____
- ❖ _____
- ❖ _____
- ❖ _____

Mate 2 – Sex Toys List

Date: _____

- ❖ _____
- ❖ _____
- ❖ _____
- ❖ _____
- ❖ _____
- ❖ _____

Week 4 - Love Making Spots - Replay

It is time to explore love making spots again – Take a look at your list from the first month and pick a spot or look for additional spots to explore.

There is still time to do some research on the internet. Go to Google Search and type in "Places to have sex" to retrieve tons of ideas. Dig deep into your thoughts for that fantasy land that all of us have.

Suggestions:
- At a friend's house – trying to stay quiet
- In a store bathroom
- On the wash machine when it is on spin cycle

Have sex in one spot from each person's list this week.

The week is dedicated to tapping into your daring side.

Mate 1 – Love Making Spots and Descriptions - Replay

Date: _____

❖ _____
   _____
   _____

❖ _____
   _____
   _____

Mate 2 – Love Making Spots and Descriptions - Replay

Date: _____

❖ _____
   _____
   _____

❖ _____
   _____
   _____

Month 11

Did you enjoy last month?

Are you ready for another fantastic month of activities?

If you are ready, turn the page and let the spice begin!

Are you Ready to Date?

Did you enjoy your dates last month?

It is time to plan your next dates. Use your creative imagination when planning the ideal date. Go to Google Search and type in "ideal date night" to retrieve tons of ideas.

Suggestions:

- Walk a nature trail holding hands
- Take a dinner cruise or boat ride
- Go see a play

Concentrate on these dates and share them with your mate. Read each one together and discuss which ones to take.

Get ready to experience more exciting dates.

Mate 1 – Dates for the Month

First Date

Date: _____ Time: _____

Destination: _____

Second Date

Date: _____ Time: _____

Destination: _____

Mate 2 – Dates for the Month

First Date

Date: _____ Time: _____

Destination: _____

Second Date

Date: _____ Time: _____

Destination: _____

Week 1 - Call Me from Another Room

Do you remember when you stayed on the phone till you fell asleep? The next day neither one of you could remember everything talked about.

In this exercise each person will write down ideas of what to talk about on the phone with your mate. The call cannot be work related.

Suggestions:
- What turns me on about you
- What I really like about you

Concentrate on conversations to have with your mate to tap into the spice.

This week is dedicated to bringing back that loving feeling and that initial spark.

Mate 1 – Call Me from Another Room

Date: _____

- ❖ _____
- ❖ _____
- ❖ _____
- ❖ _____
- ❖ _____
- ❖ _____

Mate 2 – Call Me from Another Room

Date: _____

- ❖ _____
- ❖ _____
- ❖ _____
- ❖ _____
- ❖ _____
- ❖ _____
- ❖ _____

Week 2 - Attraction through Media

When have you ever displayed your attraction to your mate through the media?

Write down songs, poems etc. that convey your attraction to you mate.

Refer back to first exercise in journal Attraction

Suggestions:

- You are so beautiful – Joe Cocker
- 100 Ways – James Ingram
- Two Occasions – The deal
- Sexual Healing – Marvin Gaye

Concentrate on what you want to convey to your mate through a medium.

Send you mate a message through song, poetry or other medium this week.

The week is dedicated to tapping into your musical or poetic romantic communicative side.

Mate 1 – Attraction Through Media

Date: _____

- ❖ _____
- ❖ _____
- ❖ _____
- ❖ _____
- ❖ _____
- ❖ _____

Mate 2 – Attraction Through Media

Date: _____

- ❖ _____
- ❖ _____
- ❖ _____
- ❖ _____
- ❖ _____
- ❖ _____

Week 3 - Cuddle Time

When was the last time you cuddled up with your partner?

Write down places to have some close cuddle time with your mate.

Suggestions:

- Floor with blanket
- Couch
- At the movies

Concentrate on places to experience cuddle time with your mate.

Cuddle with your mate in some of the places on their list.

The week is dedicated to tapping into loving closeness.

Mate 1 – Attraction Through Media

Date: _____

- ❖ _____
- ❖ _____
- ❖ _____
- ❖ _____
- ❖ _____
- ❖ _____

Mate 2 – Attraction Through Media

Date: _____

- ❖ _____
- ❖ _____
- ❖ _____
- ❖ _____
- ❖ _____
- ❖ _____

Week 4 - Undress Me

Have you ever undressed your partner?

Write down ways to undress your partner.

Suggestions:

- Undress with your eyes
- Music while undressing
- Playing a game to win a piece of clothing
- Dance for them – to win a piece of clothing that you can remove

Concentrate on exciting ways to undress your mate.

The week is dedicated to tapping into your imagination and creativity.

Mate 1 – Attraction Through Media

Date: _____

- ❖ _____
- ❖ _____
- ❖ _____
- ❖ _____
- ❖ _____
- ❖ _____

Mate 2 – Attraction Through Media

Date: _____

- ❖ _____
- ❖ _____
- ❖ _____
- ❖ _____
- ❖ _____
- ❖ _____
- ❖ _____

Month 12

Did you enjoy last month?

Are you ready for another fantastic month of activities?

If you are ready, turn the page and let the spice begin!

Are you Ready to Date?

Did you enjoy your dates last month?

It is time to plan your next dates. Use your creative imagination when planning the ideal date. Go to Google Search and type in "ideal date night" to retrieve tons of ideas.

Suggestions:

- Go skating
- Get all wet at a waterpark
- Have brunch together at a place you have never eaten before

Concentrate on these dates and share them with your mate. Read each one together and discuss which ones to take.

Get ready to experience more exciting dates.

Mate 1 – Dates for the Month

First Date

Date: _____   Time: _____

Destination: _____

Second Date

Date: _____   Time: _____

Destination: _____

Mate 2 – Dates for the Month

First Date

Date: _____   Time: _____

Destination: _____

Second Date

Date: _____   Time: _____

Destination: _____

Week 1 - Love Making Spots - Replay

It is time to explore love making spots again – Take a look at your list from the first month and pick a spot or look for additional spots to explore.

There is still time to do some research on the internet. Go to Google Search and type in "Places to have sex" to retrieve tons of ideas. Dig deep into your thoughts for that fantasy land that all of us have.

Suggestions:
- Under the water sprinkler outside
- In the garage on the hood of the car
- Sneak into house showing and go into an empty room

Have sex in one spot from each person's list this week.

The week is dedicated to tapping into your daring side.

Mate 1 – Love Making Spots and Descriptions - Replay

Date: _____

- ❖ _____
  _____
  _____

- ❖ _____
  _____
  _____

Mate 2 – Love Making Spots and Descriptions - Replay

Date: _____

- ❖ _____
  _____
  _____

- ❖ _____
  _____
  _____

Week 2 - Love Making Positions – Replay

It is time to explore love making positions again – Take a look at your list from the first month and pick a spot or look for additional spots to explore.

Research is available on the internet. Go to Google Search and type in "sex position" to retrieve tons of ideas. Dig deep into your thoughts for that fantasy land that all of us have.

Suggestions:

- Banana Split – You are on your belly. Your partner thrusts into you from behind lifting your hips.
- Couch Dance - Get on your knees in front of the couch and drape your torso over the cushions in a sort of modified doggie. Your partner enters from behind. Add vibrating cock ring for added pleasure.

Explore some positions on your list or some new positions.

The week is dedicated to tapping into your put the motion in ocean side.

Mate 1 – Love Making Positions - Replay

Date: _____

- ❖ _____
  _____
- ❖ _____
  _____

Mate 2 – Love Making Position - Replay

Date: _____

- ❖ _____
  _____
- ❖ _____
  _____

Week 3 - Role Play - Replay

It is time to role-play again – Take a look at your list from the first month and pick a role or look for additional roles.

Remember the Example. You be the doctor and your mate be the patient and you have to examine every part of their body to make sure they are okay. You use tools to explore and explain as you go. You use your own made up technical terms to bring the most excitement to your partner.

There is still time to do some research on the internet. Go to Google and enter 'Sexual role play' for tons of ideals. Dig deep into your thoughts for that fantasy land that all of us have.

Suggestions:
- Landlord – Renter
- Sex Therapist – Patient – what tricks can the therapist teach.
- Personal Trainer – Client – What workouts can you teach the new client

Practice one role from each person this week.

The week is dedicated to re-tapping into your creativity and wild side.

Mate 1 – Role Play – Replay

What are your choices? New? First Month?

Date: _____

❖ _____
   _____

❖ _____
   _____

Mate 2 – Role Play – Replay

What are your choices? New? First Month?

Date: _____

❖ _____
   _____

❖ _____
   _____

Week 4 - Keeping your Relationship Spicy Recap

Has this guided journal spiced up your relationship?

The purpose of this exercise is to continue that spiciness throughout your relationship.

The journal can be repeated in its entirety or pieces at any time.

In this exercise.

- Write down the top 5 things in the journal that spiced up your relationship
- Write down up to 5 things you thought about doing that was not in the journal

This week enjoy one of the top 5 things that spiced up your relationship or one of the new items.

Email the top 5 that were not in the journal to the author at info@booksbyAnnetteC.com, to be entered into a chance to win a free autographed copy of the next journal.

5 Spices in Journal

Date: _____

- ❖ _____
- ❖ _____
- ❖ _____
- ❖ _____
- ❖ _____
- ❖ _____

5 Spices – Not in Journal

Date: _____

- ❖ _____
- ❖ _____
- ❖ _____
- ❖ _____
- ❖ _____
- ❖ _____

About the Author

Annette Crittenden has had a love for writing book, plays, and manuals since she was in grade school. Coming from a loving home she always wanted everyone to experience the same.

Although she did not see a lot of the things she writes about in her home, her imagination made her think of the things that could have been happening behind the close doors. Her mom and dad always came out smiling.

At an early age she would spend hours and hours in every book she could find. She found it was a way to take people to places that they have never been in their mind. She found that writing was a way to help people improve their life.

She started writing poetry and love letters for her friends to give to their mates. She writes everything from poems for funerals to poems for birthdays and weddings.

Annette and her husband promised each other 50 years of marriage. For 50 years of marriage there has to be away to keep it interesting, loving, forgiving, and spicy. Sharing the loving and spicy journey is what inspired her to start publishing journals and novels.

Keeping Your Relationship Spicy is her debut journal. Look forward to years of novels and journals in the future.

Find out more:
www.BooksByAnnetteC.com

Made in the USA
Coppell, TX
17 May 2020